CLOISTER

BOOKS

Cloister Books are inspired by the monastic custom of reading as one walks slowly in the monastery cloister—a place of silence, centering, and calm. Within these pages you will find a similar space in which to pray and reflect on the presence of God.

Cowley Publications is a ministry of the brothers of the Society of Saint John the Evangelist, a monastic order in the Episcopal Church. Our mission is to provide books and resources for those seeking spiritual and theological formation. Cowley Publications is committed to developing a new generation of writers and teachers who will encourage people to think and pray in new ways about spirituality, reconciliation, and the future.

Parting Words

Parting Words

A farewell discourse

Barbara Clementine Harris

Cowley Publications
Cambridge, Massachusetts

Published in the United States of America by Cowley Publications, a division of the Society of Saint John the Evangelist. No portion of this book may be reproduced, stored in or introduced into a retrieval system, or transmitted, in any form or by any means-including photocopying-without the prior written permission of Cowley Publications, except in the case of brief quotations embedded in critical articles and reviews.

Library of Congress Cataloging-in-Publication Data:
Harris, Barbara C. (Barbara Clementine)
    Parting words : a farewell discourse / Barbara Clementine Harris.
        p. cm.
Includes bibliographical references.
    ISBN 1-56101-217-3 (pbk. : alk. paper)
    1. Episcopal Church—Sermons. 2. Anglican Communion—Sermons. 3. African American women clergy. 4. Sermons, American—20th century. I. Title.
BX5937.A3H37 2003
252'.03—dc21
                                2003013522

Scripture quotations are taken from *The New Revised Standard Version of the Bible,* © 1989, by the Division of Christian Education of the National Council of the Churches of Christ in the United States of America. Used by permission.

Cover design: Gary Ragaglia

This book was printed by Transcontinental Printing in Canada on acid-free paper.

Cowley Publications
907 Massachusetts Avenue
Cambridge, Massachusetts 02139
800-225-1534 • www.cowleypublications.org

To the memory of the Reverend Paul
Matthews Washington, rector, mentor,
teacher, and friend, who embraced in his life—
and encouraged me to hear and heed—
the Apostle's admonition to
"speak the truth in love."

TABLE OF CONTENTS

Foreword • Parting Words—Not Last Words
by the Right Reverend John B. Chane,
Bishop of Washington . . . 9

I • "Peace! Be Still!" . . . 13

II • Wise Investments . . . 23

III • A Thirst for the Kingdom . . . 33

IV • A Ready Remnant . . . 47

V • Looking for a Savior . . . 55

VI • Easter Grace in a Good Friday World . . . 67

VII • Costly Friendship . . . 75

VIII • Parting Words . . . 83

Afterword • The Power Behind—The Task Ahead . . . 95

Foreword

Parting Words—
Not Last Words

From the very first day of her ministry among us as a bishop in Christ's Holy, catholic, Apostolic Church, the Right Reverend Barbara Clementine Harris has been a prophetic voice, preaching the Gospel and unashamedly proclaiming the good news of God in Christ to a church, culture, and world too often caught up in the brokenness of the human heart, soul, and mind.

Parting Words is a collection of sermons Bishop Harris preached before various congregations and communities in the Episcopal Diocese of Massachusetts during the year preceding her retirement as bishop suffragan. These sermons are vintage Barbara Harris. They speak of her unshakable and unbroken faith in Jesus Christ. *Parting Words* gives life to familiar stories, places, and people in scripture and allows the reader to experience in a very intimate way the theology of one of the church's truly great preachers.

None can escape the deep roots of Barbara's personal journey as it is contained in these pages. Much of her journey is defined in reference to the great gospel hymns and spirituals of the African American church and powerfully amplified by sermons preached about salvation and sacrifice, oppression and freedom, and speaking the Gospel's truth to power. Barbara stands with the great women of the Bible who loved their God passion-

10

ately and who proudly bore the marks of their conversion and faithfulness.

Although Barbara has retired from the Diocese of Massachusetts, possibly as its most beloved bishop suffragan, her prophetic voice will continue to cry out within the life of the larger church as she continues preaching and teaching in the Diocese of Washington, D.C. *Parting Words* reminds us that Barbara never really belonged to the church, let alone to the world. For Barbara Harris has always belonged to Jesus. And this collection invites all of us to join her in that relationship.

John B. Chane, Bishop of Washington

I

"Peace! Be Still!"

*An address to the Diocesan Convention,
Boston, Massachusetts, November 2001*

Mark 4:35–41

"Jesus woke up and rebuked the wind and said to the sea, 'Peace! Be still!' Then the wind ceased, and there was a dead calm. He said to the disciples, 'Why are you afraid? Have you still no faith?' And they were filled with great awe and said to one another, 'Who then is this, that even wind and sea obey him'?"

How many times recently have you said or heard someone say, "I don't feel like watching the news. It's all bad anyhow?" In the midst of uncertainty and swift transition, in the midst of personal and institutional upheaval, and amid the "fightings within and fears without" that separate peoples, races, and nations, we desperately need to hear a little good news. And this passage from the fourth chapter of Mark's gospel, which relates how Jesus calmed the storm on the Sea of Galilee, is exactly that: good news.

Who among us, having been on a boat when a squall came up, having flown on a plane through extreme turbulence, or having lived through a tornado, hurricane, or even a violent thunderstorm, can fail to be moved by this account of the terror-stricken disciples, convinced that at any moment their boat would capsize and they would be swept away into the sea. And who could fail to be moved by the image of Jesus standing up in that frail vessel and speaking to the storm: "'Peace! Be still.'

Then the winds ceased, and there was a dead calm."

This story has inspired beautiful paintings of Jesus in the prow of the boat, his arms outstretched as he commands the angry waters and the raging wind to cease, be still. It has inspired hymn writers to fashion into poetry and gospel song their awe and wonder at the power of the Son of God. And through their poetry and music, we can feel God's power to rule and order not only the unruly wills and affections of sinners, but the universe as well.

We all know people who, with much zeal, try to explain the so-called "nature miracles," this and other stories that immediately follow in Mark's gospel: Jesus' casting out the mob of demons from the tormented man and driving them into a herd of swine; his healing the woman who had been severely hemorrhaging for twelve years; the raising of Jairus's daughter from the dead. People try to explain these miracles using naturalistic theories or rationalistic methods. They seek to probe the coincidences, the circumstances, and the probabilities of the situation.

Bible commentary tells us we should leave these stories where they stand. I would add further that picking them apart makes them more a burden on our faith in the presence and power of God than a support to it. It is unfortunate that some people's faith has become so weak and so watered down that they have to rationalize and explain away the power of God as manifested in Jesus, the Christ. There are some people who try to give you scientific explanations of how that storm ceased. We need a return to and renew that old-fashioned faith in which the miracles were not quite as stupendous to those who experienced or reported them as they often seem to us today.

Some time ago I spent several hours visiting with about 125 men in the recovery unit of a county jail. At one point they began to sing hymns, and one of them was Andre Crouch's gospel song: "Take me back, dear Lord to the place where I first received you. Take me back to the place where I first believed." Well might that be *our* song: Take me back. Take me back to childlike trust; take me back to a lively faith; take me back to eager hope. That song echoes and even older song of supplication: "Create in me a clean heart, O God, and renew a right spirit within me." (Ps. 51:10, *BCP*)

For early Christians, miracles did not contravene any natural law. They were the natural law to those who believed in Jesus Christ. Again, Bible commentary and historians remind us, "for them, the importance was not so much in the miracle itself, but in what the miracle reiterated about the presence, the power, and the saving purpose of God."

But we can understand the disciples out there on the sea. They were in a state of panic. They cried out to Jesus like frightened children. Don't you care that we are about to die? How can you lie there asleep?

They were trying to communicate their distress and their fear to Jesus. What they did not understand, and what many today do not understand is that although we may panic in times of stress and distress, God does not share our panic.

That sense of panic that gripped the disciples out there on the Sea of Galilee is pervasive in our church and in our society today. When people panic, they tend to act desperately and unreasonably. Nations panic and go to war. Then they try to get God to sanction their actions as "holy." In panic, people choose up sides in controversies and take irrational stands. Entire groups of people are singled out. They become targets of hatred, contempt, and oppression because of their race, gender, class, sexual orientation, or economic status. Few, if any, say, "Come, let us reason together."

In every phase of our lives panic gets acted out. We fail to wait for that still small voice of calm, the voice Elijah heard when, in panic, he fled for his life, escaping to the caves of the wilderness. Elijah did not hear the voice of God in the fury of wind, earthquake, or fire. He heard it in a whisper.

We have put our hope in secular solutions to situations of human distress. Seldom are these solutions fashioned in an atmosphere of calm reason or quiet trust. We act as though secular solutions and temporal remedies are the only resources available to us. We need to wait on God. We need to center down, be still, and know that God is God and that God does all things well.

The bottom line for us is that we are all in the same boat, and if we panic, we could capsize. If we recognize that, we can confront danger, adversity, and tribulation of any kind. We can know that if we trust in him, Jesus can calm the storms of our lives. But we must call on him as did the disciples.

If Christ is at the center of our lives, we don't have to rush into irrational action that often leads to impractical solutions. "Peace! Be still!" These can be our watchwords as we wait for the guidance and direction of the Holy Spirit.

Often as we sail over the tempestuous sea of

life, our world is in storm on a personal, national, and global level. But not only is Christ on the ship, Christ is in command—even when he seems to be asleep. "He who keeps watch over Israel will neither slumber nor sleep." (Ps. 121:3, *BCP*) And what a comfort lies in the simple thought: "His eye is on the sparrow and I know he watches me."

Jesus hears us when we call, but he refuses to jump when we push the panic button. We are afraid to rely on that presence and the saving power. In our haste and our anxiety, we tend to rely on what we can see, count, touch, and feel. We forget that such things will pass away. We need, in the words of the old hymn, to "build our hopes on things eternal and hold to God's unchanging hand."

Yes, we may come in panic like those fearful disciples in the boat saying:

Master, the tempest is raging,
The billows are tossing high,

"Peace! Be Still!"

The sky is o'er shadowed with blackness,
No shelter, nor haven is nigh.
Carest thou not that we perish?
How can'st thou lie asleep,
When each moment so madly is threatening
A grave in the angry deep?

But it is in faith that we hear and trust the response:

The winds and the waves shall obey
my will: Peace! Be still!
Whether the wrath of a storm-tossed sea,
Or demons, or men, or whatever it be,
No water can swallow the ship where lies
The master of ocean and earth and skies,
They all shall sweetly obey my will:
Peace! Peace! Be still. (Mary A. Baker)

II

Wise Investments

A sermon on stewardship

Matthew 6:21

As you can imagine, I have heard and preached my own share of stewardship homilies, and *you* have heard enough of them to know that they usually begin with the story of the "widow's mite" or some such story of self-sacrifice. But I am reminded of a modern-day parable, the source of which I do not know, concerning a conversation between a one hundred dollar bill and a one dollar bill.

The one hundred dollar bill said to the one dollar bill, "I have been with the jet set to Las Vegas, Monte Carlo, the Riviera and to all the great casinos of the world. Where, indeed, have you been?" The one dollar bill humbly replied, "Oh, I too have made the rounds. I've been to Saint John's, Saint Andrew's, Saint Gabriel's, Grace, and Saint Luke's." Please feel free to add the name of any church that comes to mind. I want to say something about investing, investing wisely, and specifically, investing in the church.

We all are conscious of investments whether or not we personally hold any. We also are conscious of returns on investments, especially in a volatile economic climate, and certainly the stock market has done its share of fluctuating in recent months.

Earlier this year, I looked at an "intelligence report" from one of my brokerage houses. It was full of optimism, but it was also replete with disclaimers, cautionary notes, and a healthy share of double-talk. The report presented "new opportunities for your portfolio." It said the "new" consumer who is likely to be "older and wiser"—neither the ebullient youth of the 1960s nor the conspicuous consumer of the 1980s. The report went on to say some other things—not all was surprising, and most was understandable. For example, it said "income should rise faster than consumption as the savings rate rises," a plus for firms that offer financial services to affluent consumers.

With or without such pertinent "intelligence," there are some things we instinctively know about the investment climate and the investment market. We know that with the exception, perhaps, of municipal and other reputable bonds, investing means generally high risk. It can be highly speculative, and it is subject to fluctuation with encouraging increases and discouraging declines. Moreover, the market—as we have witnessed on such occasions as "Black Monday" a few years ago—can crash. (I do wish they could have come up with a better descriptor for that financial debacle: I'm really weary of my color being associated with everything bad that happens in this world.) The bottom line and the one thing we all understand about the market is this: a return on our investment is not guaranteed.

Well, investing in the church has some of the same characteristics. The apostle Paul and those active in the early church came to know that all too well: the risks were high; the enterprise was highly speculative; participation in the venture was subject to fluctuation; and there were encouraging increases and discouraging declines.

Only the bottom line proved to be different. There was, and there is, a guaranteed return—not one that necessarily was realized in their lifetime, nor one that is readily evident in terms we today like to calculate, measure or see as success. But there is the guaranteed return in terms of the kingdom. There is the guaranteed return of grace: what old folks sometimes refer to as "free grace, undying love."

The great abolitionist Frederick Douglas once said, "You don't get everything you pay for, but you pay for everything you get." And while we cannot argue the basic and existential truth of that statement, there is one thing about which it is not true—and that is grace. Grace, as we know, is unearned, unmerited, and undeserved. While it is freely given, grace is not without some requisite response from us. That response is thanksgiving.

In thanksgiving we are invited to invest ourselves in the work of kingdom building. This is what Saint Paul refers to in the Second Letter to Timothy: "As for you . . . do the work of an evangelist, carry out your ministry fully." (2 Tim. 4:5) Notice I left out the good part that says "always be sober, endure suffering."

What does investing in the church really mean? There are several definitions of the word "invest" in dictionary, but I was struck by one which says "to use, give, or devote time, talent, etc. with the expectation of some satisfaction." Now that opens up all kinds of possibilities!

We are invited, for example, to invest in the lives of children—our posterity. We are invited to come face-to-face with the stark and harsh realities lived by so many children in our society today. And we are invited to invest time, money, and effort in advocacy and action for making a significant change in their lives. We are reminded that ours is a society in which more than a million latchkey children come home to houses in which there are guns.

Moreover, every day in America five children or teens commit suicide; nine children or teens are homicide victims; thirty-four children or teens die from accidents; 180 children are arrested for violent crimes; 1,329 babies are born without health insurance; 2,851 high school students drop out; and 7,883 children are reported abused or neglected. I repeat, everyday in America! These grim statistics relate not only to the inner-city communities of major cities. They reflect what can and does happen in affluent suburban communities as well. We are invited to enter into the lives of our children in a meaningful way, providing opportunities for them to flourish and for each of them to reach his or her full potential.

If we truly invest in the lives of our young people, who are among the most vulnerable in our society, we will invest ourselves in other areas as well. We will invest in peace with justice so that the "swords" of civil unrest might indeed "be beaten into plowshares" and its "spears into pruning hooks" at home and abroad. We will invest in pastoral outreach among people who may never enter our churches as parishioners or even visitors to our worship. We will invest in prophetic witness. A witness that advocates on behalf of the poor, the powerless, and the marginalized. A witness that questions the unquestioned and challenges the unchallenged notions of class and privilege in our society.

We will invest in the wider mission of the church, engaging ourselves in areas of public life beyond the borders of our parishes and our diocese and working to lift up the least, the lost, and the left out. We will invest in congregational development that points us beyond numbers toward richer, inter-generational life together: life in which we are sensitive to the needs, cares, and concerns of each other—no matter how old we are.

Individually we will invest in our own spiritual growth and development, an outcome of which can be a more focused prayer life that lifts the concerns of others before God. We will invest in the kingdom, the *shalom,* the peace of God's reign.

Why, some will ask, should I invest myself in a church so fraught with conflict and dissension, sometimes with scandal, and with what some regard as lackluster leadership and other problems? Why invest in a church that, for others, seems to have lost its spiritual moorings, its moral authority, and its prophetic voice. Still others ask why should I invest in a church that seems exclusionary rather than inclusive?

Some of these criticisms are rooted in truth, but we need to remember what the church really is. The church is not just its national headquarters or General Convention or Executive Council between conventions. The church in Massachusetts is not just its bishops and diocesan staff. The church is not just issues of human sexuality, women's ordination, or liturgical revision; nor is it the other divisions and diversions that distract us from our mission. The church is not even the Lambeth Conference—its decennial gathering of bishops from throughout the Anglican Communion, which really is small potatoes in the larger Christian world.

The church is all this, but it is and can be so much more. It is and ought to be the people of God serving the people of God; people loving and caring for each other; people celebrating joys and sharing sorrows; people bearing not only one another's burdens, but also literally bearing each other. As the Body of Christ, the church is and ought to be a safe haven of refuge where nobody is abused or exploited. It must be an inclusive fellowship where nobody is an outcast. We, the church, are called to be the wounded, loving hands of Jesus in a troubled world.

Such an enterprise is worth our investment. It is worth the investment of our time, our talent, and our treasure, for, as scripture tells us, "where your treasure is, there will your heart be also." (Mt. 6:21).

III

A Thirst for
the Kingdom

A sermon on longing and desire

John 4:5-26

In the fourth chapter of John's gospel, we have an
interesting story that begins with a little verbal
sparring between Jesus and a woman who has come
to draw water from the well of Jacob. She is seeking
something more than water. Most of use are as well,
so as we put this encounter into focus and context,
join me as we ponder what it is to thirst for God, to

thirst for the Kingdom of God.

With this detailed description of the encounter between Jesus and the Samaritan woman, I am mindful of the fact that usually, when we consider examples of feminine faithfulness, we hold up women of unquestioned character, unblemished reputation, and solid achievement. Certainly many such women do come quickly to mind, not only from the pages of scripture, but from everyday life as well. We tend to focus on the virtues of womanhood, to highlight strengths rather than weaknesses, fine points rather than faults, and sterling qualities rather than sins. We usually hold up the "perfect," but in this text we learn from the imperfect, the broken, the outcast, from the woman of questionable character.

Jesus, on his way from Judea to Galilee, is passing through Samaria. He is passing through unfriendly territory. In those days, everyone was aware of the antagonism between Jews and Samaritans; it had existed from the time of Ezra and Nehemiah. Jews and Samaritans were separated by serious theological differences. Jews did not think much of Samaritans, who probably returned the favor. To the Jews, Samaritans were not only unclean, they were barbaric. That is why the disciples and others were so shocked when Jesus used the parable of the Good Samaritan to illustrate his answer to the question: "Who is my neighbor?" They were caught up short also by the story of the cleansing of the ten lepers, the only one of whom returned to give thanks was a Samaritan. The Jewish disciples could not imagine that Jesus would use a Samaritan as a good example of anything.

So it is odd that, although weary from his journey and the midday heat, our Lord would stop to rest in this hostile place. But Jesus, as on so many other occasions in his ministry, chooses an odd place to stop and to bear witness to and reveal the glory and love of God. Think about it: does he not still stop in the odd places of our lives today?

It was not unusual, however, that Jesus—who

often broke with tradition—would request water, even from a stranger, a member of an enemy group, a woman. Water was life sustaining in that parched and barren land. And his request was one that would not be denied, even from a sworn enemy. Life was much simpler in that time; there were certain things one simply would not deny another person—like water—in a desert climate. Scripture was (and is) very clear on hospitality to strangers. So Jesus says to this woman with her water jar, "Give me a drink."

Don't be fooled—the Lord has more than water on his mind. Jesus' resting at this physical fork in the road between Judea and Galilee on his journey to his ultimate earthly destination, Jerusalem and Calvary, is also at a spiritual crossroads. His mission is coming full circle as he makes the tortuous journey that culminates in our salvation. And he is about to do something he has not done before. Here he reveals to this woman of the hated Samaritans—this woman of questionable repute—information he has refrained from revealing to people who might be regarded as more worthy of his attention: Jesus reveals to this woman in no uncertain terms that he is Messiah.

Prior to this encounter, there have been other instances in which the Father's glory has been shown through the Son and in which Jesus carefully has told his followers that it is not yet time to lay out the full story. At the wedding feast at Cana, Jesus told his mother his hour had not yet come; on the Mount of Transfiguration, where, caught up between Moses and Elijah, Jesus shone forth in radiant beauty, but he cautioned his disciples to tell no one any of what they had been privileged to see. He gave similar admonishments along with certain of his miracles of healing. Yet here at this crossroads, Jesus makes himself known to this woman.

As if to document his revelation, he also tells this woman about herself. He blows her cover as if to reinforce the truth that before God, the secrets of all hearts are revealed. It shocks us whenever somebody sees through us and discovers what we would rather keep hidden. We go to great lengths to cover up our secrets. We make sure we are seen with the right people in the right places; we join the proper organizations and institutions, including the church.

It is human nature to try to hide and cover up the unflattering, the unattractive, the uncomfortable aspects of our lives. At first, the woman at the well tries to be cagey. She tries to dodge the question and the issue. "Go, call your husband," Jesus instructs her. She says, "I have no husband." Right, says Jesus, and he proceeds to detail her liaisons and her indiscretions. "You've had five husbands, and the man you have now is not your husband." Imagine how we would react if we were personally confronted that way by Jesus. I can hear it: "Now look here, Jesus, you done left off preachin' and gone to meddling! Will you just stick to preachin', please?"

She also challenges him when he says that if she knew who she was talking to and what God was offering her, she would be the one who would be asking, "Give me a drink." And he would give her living water. "Are you greater than our father Jacob who gave us this well?" she asks. But Jesus stays right on the case. "Everyone who drinks of this water will be thirsty again, but those who drink of the water that I will give will never be thirsty."

Ultimately this woman realizes that she is conversing with someone different from anyone she has ever met or known, someone special, somebody with something to offer, a person who could make a difference in her life. And that's what Jesus is all about: making a difference in our lives, helping us to emerge into our full stature as children of God.

I think this strange story of the woman at the well has some clear messages for us as we stand at our individual crossroads and ponder the choices of life in a vain world that is no friend to grace; messages for us as we consider ourselves emerging people of Christ's kingdom; messages for us when we, like the woman at the well, realize that while we are not yet what we should be, thank God we are not what we were. We are different because God has touched our lives; different because we realize we can learn from all God's people even from such folk as the Samaritan woman—a street woman, if you will.

No matter what you think of the Samaritan woman, a fact—and an important fact—is that she was at the well. She was there where Jesus was. Had she not gone to the well when she did, she would not have been privileged to meet and have an encounter with the Savior. No matter her reason for going at the odd hour she went (scholars tell us she was there at an unusual time—not in the early dawn nor in the cool of the evening, the times at which water was normally drawn). She had gone in the burning heat of the day, when the sun was scorching, when everybody else was looking for shade, for some relief from the midday heat. No matter her reason for going at that hour, she was at the right place at the right time. If you don't go near the well, you cannot draw water. You must make yourself present and available to receive the living water God so freely gives. You must go to the well!

Too many people are absent from the well. Because the woman came, she received a blessing. Simply because she came, she received a blessing. So many stay away and do not avail themselves of the blessings that can be theirs. People stay away for various reasons. Some like the Samaritan woman, feel scorned and derided because they lead unconventional lives. Others feel rejected because of who and what they are. Some stay away because they don't want to rub shoulders with those they consider undesirable, those who, for one reason or another, don't fit in, those who are poor or shabby or unwashed.

Some get so locked up in their own troubles— their own trials and tribulations—so trapped in that small box of self-pity, they absent themselves from the well. Some are so caught up in the pastimes and pleasures of this world, they absent themselves from the well. They sing, "Go Spirit, go Thy way, some more convenient day, on Thee I'll call."[1] Some are so puffed up with self-righteousness, they think they don't even need a drink. People have absented themselves from the well because they have not realized Jesus can give them new hearts, new minds, new songs to sing, new ways of looking at life, new ways of loving other people—even the unlovable—if they have a thirst for the Kingdom.

Another point to remember is that the Samaritan woman brought a vessel. If you have not grown up in the country or visited a rural area where folks rely on wells, you might not know about drawing water. Getting water from a well is not like cupping your hands or holding a glass under a faucet or pressing a button on a water

---

[1] From the hymn "Almost Persuaded" by Philip P. Bliss.

fountain. If you are going to make use of a well, you must bring something with which to draw water. The woman told Jesus, "Sir, you have no bucket, and the well is deep."

That is true of God's grace. Too many of us come to the well empty-handed. We have no vessel in which to draw up the living water. People say to me, "I come to church, but I don't get anything out of it." If you don't bring anything in which or with which to get something, you won't get anything. We bring to the throne of grace the thin shells of ourselves instead of open, trusting hearts and souls, vessels in which to draw up the living water. If you don't bring something you can't get anything. If you don't believe God can do something for you, you'll never know when or what God does!

Finally, the Samaritan woman not only received a blessing, she also went to tell other people. "Come see a man who told me everything I have ever done." Come and see for yourself. The woman at the well became a well woman, a *healed* woman, and she shared her wholeness with others. Too many of us do not share what has been given to us. If we would bear witness to what we have received, others might come and receive also. When was the last time you told someone that Jesus has brought you "a mighty long way."

My friends, we thirst after many things in this world. We thirst after money, power, prestige, position. We put our trust in them; we may even pray *for* them. But like our Lord, we are at a crossroads in the church and in society. We still have a choice, and the question our Lord is asking us is, "Do we have a thirst for the kingdom?"

Jesus is asking us, "Are we content to settle for the temporary thirst quenchers of life: the material values of this world, the right connections, the proper credentials, the things on which this society places so much value, things that will never slake the thirst of your parched, dry souls? Or do you thirst for righteousness, for peace, for justice, for the liberation of all God's people?

Do we thirst for those things that make for a just society as Jesus proclaimed the kingdom to be? If we gave our testimony today would we sing with the psalmist, "As the deer longs for the water-brooks, so longs my soul for you, O God"? (Ps. 42:1, *BCP*) Or would we sing with the elders: "I heard the voice of Jesus say, 'Behold, I freely give the living water; thirsty one, stoop down, and drink and live!' I came to Jesus, and I drank of that life-giving stream; my thirst was quenched, my soul revived, and now I live in him."[2]

Do we have a thirst for the living water with which God truly enriches our lives? Do we have a thirst for the kingdom? Do we have a thirst to emerge as truly faithful Christians, to be more than we are? Each of us must respond for himself or herself. Do we have a thirst for the kingdom? Jesus is patiently waiting for our answer.

---

[2] From the hymn, "I heard the voice of Jesus say" by Horatio Bonar.

IV

A Ready Remnant

A sermon for the Order of Saint Anne on their patronal feast, at Bethany Convent, Arlington, Massachusetts

1 Samuel 2:1-8; Ephesians 1:3-6, 11-12; Luke 1:26-33

The readings for this day of celebration and the portions of scripture from which they are taken speak of response and commitment to God: Hannah's thanksgiving, the apostle Paul's exhortation to the church at Ephesus, and Mary's "yes" to the pronouncement that she would be the God-bearer was, "Let it be to me according to your word." And what we know of Holy Anne, mother of the Blessed Virgin Mary, comes to us largely through legend and the tradition of the Church rather than scriptural reference. We are told of her saintly life. It is said that one day as Anne was praying under a laurel tree, an angel appeared to her and declared that God had heard her prayers. She would have a child who would be praised throughout the world. Anne replied, "As my God lives, if I conceive, the child will be a gift to my God, serving him in holiness throughout the whole of its life."

Response and commitment. Thanksgiving and faithful reaction in gratitude for the blessings bestowed by God in God's infinite mercy, love, and grace. What shining examples! What roles to follow. What marks for our own lives. Here at Bethany Convent, dwell these good sisters, whose lives of fidelity over the years have been beacons for many of us. As their situation and circumstances have been altered by time, these sisters have continued in faithful service, finding new ways to be in ministry to and with the people of God in this corner of the vineyard.

Response and commitment. Thanksgiving and faithful reaction. Fine, you say, for Paul, dramatically converted on the Damascus road. Fine, you say, for Mary, highly favored and blessed of God among women and for Mary's holy mother, who was blessed with a child after being unable to conceive. Fine, you say, for these good sisters who live under vows and chosen vocation. But what of us who dwell in a complex, vain world that is no friend to grace? What will help us on to God? What can we learn from these lives recalled for us today in scripture and in living witness?

None of those who were chosen by God for a particular purpose or service could be said to have had lives marked by ease or pleasure: the barren Hannah, year after year provoked and ridiculed by her husband's other wife because she bore no sons. Hannah and Anne, looked upon by their communities with scorn and blamed for the rejection of their husbands' earnest sacrifices to the Lord. Paul, who endured shipwreck, beatings, and imprisonment to bear witness to the good news of Jesus Christ. To say nothing of Mary who, having found favor with God, experienced such uncertainty of life and trials of the heart and soul that many today would be reluctant to claim it was God's favor. Yet in each of these lives chosen by God we know there were the key elements of firm belief and fidelity: a willingness to endure and a sense of purpose and thanksgiving that was translated into active response. They serve as constant reminders that with God, nothing is impossible. This wonderful God of testing and surprise; this wonderful God who raised up what had been cast down; this wonderful God who says to us even today: with me all things are possible, if you only believe.

There are those among us who have had more than their fair share of heartaches and heartbreaks; those whose souls and bodies have been tried; those for whom the journey has been arduous and sometimes lonely. There are those among us who have experienced mountaintop joys that quickly became wilderness woes and have known the paradoxical peaks and valleys of human existence.

There are others among us whose lives have been marked by privilege and an absence of tribulation and misfortune. For them, bitter endurance may be difficult to comprehend or even to imagine. Indeed, there are some—none of *us*, of course—who, even in this day and age, believe that good fortune is a sign of righteousness. Folk such as these not unlike those who asked Jesus, "Rabbi, who sinned, this man or his parents, that he was born blind?" (Jn. 9:2) I think you can see where I am going with this. Most, if not all, of you could stand up and finish this homily for me because you know our responsibility as God's own creation.

But these days response and commitment, thanksgiving and faithful response are in somewhat short supply. It is easier to pay the lip service of thanksgiving and praise to God than to live the

words of the old African-American spiritual:
"Done made my vow to the Lord, and I will go, I
shall go; to see what the end will be." One reason
why lip-service seems easier is that a faithful and
faith-filled response to the Gospel is not very welcome these days. Much of what is propounded as
faithful response is marked by a narrow and exclu-
sive delineation that defines who is inside and who
is outside the circle of God's loving embrace. A
more inclusive interpretation of the good news of
Jesus Christ has been called untraditional and un-
orthodox. And the bold move from charity to justice is seen as "revisionist."

What I am suggesting is that each of us is
called to make a faithful commitment to God
through our Lord and Savior, Jesus Christ. As
Christ's hands and feet in this world, we are called
to live into his promise that "I came that they may
have life and have it abundantly." (Jn. 10:10) To
live that promise, each of us must consciously and
intentionally offer ourselves to his service—not for

ourselves, but also on behalf of others.

Recently, at their commencement, I urged the graduates of one of our seminaries to consider themselves part of the remnant of God suggested by the prophet Isaiah. They should strive to be part of that tenacious band of people who will support us when we try to live the Gospel, sing the Lord's song with us in a strange land, and share a vision of the future with us. And I offer the same challenge to all of us gathered here today. But in closing let me tell you something I believe about this remnant.

Lowliness, humility, and suffering are the lot of the remnant of God in any age, including our own. But through weakness, God's strength and victory will be perfected in a rich harvest of redeemed and liberated humanity.

As it moves into the years ahead, the remnant must be willing to be used, shaped, and reshaped by God's Holy Spirit. God's remnant in the twenty-first century may not be the same, perhaps, as it was in the first century or even in the 80s or the 90s. We human beings are earthen vessels. And as the prophet Jeremiah reminds us, "The vessel he was making of clay was spoiled in the potter's hand, and he reworked it into another vessel, as seemed good to him." (Jer. 18:4) History teaches us, according to James Russell Lowell's once-familiar hymn, that "new occasions teach new duties" and that "time makes ancient good uncouth."[1]

My sisters and brothers, my message to you this day is simply this. The remnant of God lives, looks, speaks, and commits to the future: in the minds of those who understand the struggle, in the hearts of those who have dedicated their lives, in the hopes of the people for whom it is waged, and in the strength of those who will carry it out.

With Hannah, Paul, Mary, Holy Anne, and these faithful sisters, who serve with them in Christ's name, pray to be in that number.

---

[1] From the hymn, "Once to every man and nation."

V

Looking for a Savior

A sermon on seeking the presence
of Christ in our lives today

Luke 4:17b–19,21

We reflect on the state of the world today and all that is happening around us at home and abroad; the chaos and confusion that confront us daily; and our seeming inability to stem the madness that threatens to engulf our society, and we realize that this is a time for sober reflection. It is a time not only to consider our personal state of being, but a time also to ponder the human condition. It is a time of questioning, a time of searching, a time of looking for answers. So think with me on the subject: looking for a Savior.

In her later years, my grandmother Mattie was in the habit of storing most of the nice gifts she received at Christmas, and other occasions, in boxes up in the top of her closet. It seemed to me that she operating on the theory that some things were just too good to use routinely and should be saved for special times or special events. One box, which contained some beautiful lingerie was marked "Mattie's burial things." My grandmother died at age 93, leaving boxes full of unused gifts, some of which—including the burial things—were full of dry rot. Why do I tell this story? Certainly not to belittle my grandmother, who was one of the greatest women I have known, but to illustrate a point.

In the book of Revelation, John speaks of Jesus as "the one who is, who was, and who is to come." We celebrate Jesus' birth, and we spend a lot of time talking about Jesus of Nazareth, the one who was. We bury our loved ones in the sure and certain hope of the Resurrection, promised by the one who is to come again. But what about the one who *is*? We claim to have a faith and we talk about our faith, but so many of us live with a faith full of unused gifts like those in my grandmother's boxes. These gifts are the Savior's promises of power for living now—today.

Sunday after Sunday we stand and confess our faith as contained in the Creed: "We believe in one God, the Father, the Almighty. . . ." And we sing of our faith in wonderful hymns: "My faith looks up to thee, thou lamb of Calvary, Savior divine." But for many of us these are only words repeated in worship; they are not a reality in our lives. Come Monday morning, many of us face life as if Jesus were not present.

Every morning all of us wake up to a world in crisis and pain. We wake up also to our own personal responsibilities, decisions, opportunities, and problems. We wake up to our own cares and woes, our own joys and sorrows, and our own emotional and physical pains. And perhaps we may wonder whether faith is meant to be an every-day source of strength. For some of us, there is a litany of questions. First we ask, "Will I make it through?" Next we ask, "How can I make it through?" Then we get to the really pitiable ques-tion, "Is there no help for me?" We are not the first to ask. The ancient prophet Habakkuk pleaded "O Lord, how long shall I cry for help, and you will not listen? Or cry to you 'Violence!' and you will not save?" (Hab. 1:2) Jeremiah asked, "Is there no balm in Gilead? Is there no physician there?" (Jer. 8:22)

People the world over are asking the same questions today. The answer comes back to us as it has to seekers over the centuries. The answer comes back to us as it came to my forbears, in their great affirmations of faith that we have received as "spirituals." Even as they were bowed under the cruel yoke of slavery, they could sing with confidence, "There is a balm in Gilead to make the wounded whole." The answer comes to us from the cross of Calvary, and it echoes out of the empty tomb. We, too, live in a time of questioning, a time of seeking answers, a time of looking. People are looking for a savior. People are looking for some savior. But that does not mean they are looking for the *Savior*.

People look in strange places for their salvation. That is not new either. False gods and false idols have been around for a long time. Joshua had to call the Israelites back to remembrance. In his farewell address to the troops, he admonished them: "Choose this day whom you will serve, whether the gods your ancestors served in the region beyond the River or the gods of the Amorites in whose land you are living; but as for me and my household, we will serve the Lord." (Josh. 24:15) The prophet Elijah had his "showdown" at Mount Carmel with the priests of Baal, and he proved whose god had the power to save. We still have our share of false gods and idols.

Folk put their faith and trust in a lot of things they think can save them—fame, fortune, prestige, power, family, the right partner, the right job, the right house—in the right neighborhood. They pray about them; they even pray *for* them. You know well what I'm talking about.

Money. Lord, if I could just get my hands on enough money to get out of this hole I'm in right now, everything would be all right. Reverend Ike, noted radio evangelist, was fond of saying, "The only thing money can't buy is poverty." Don't you believe it. That's a lie. Money can buy you some things you not only don't want or need, it can also buy you some things that can kill you. It can buy you a fast round-trip to hell and back. Ask the folk whose money has bought them an addiction to crack cocaine, heroin, or some other drug.(And somehow we have *got to* communicate that to our young people—those who sell drugs as well as those who use them. Like the users, the sellers, even in affluent communities, are flirting with death. And the money they make may look good, but it's not in their pockets long enough to do them any good. It is only a drop in the bucket compared with what those who flood our communities with that junk make out of the drug deals. Neither money nor the fleeting "highs" one gets from drugs can save anyone.

Folks put their trust in having the right connections, in knowing the right people. They have no confidence in their own God-given gifts and abilities to persevere to the end, so they think they have to make the right connections under the rubric "it's not what you know, but who you know." In the long run, the so-called right connections don't really mean all that much. There is an old saying: "If you can produce, your enemies can't hurt you. If you can't produce, your friends can't help you." And there is much truth in that.

Some put their trust in position, a point from

which they can "wheel and deal." Some trust power, others sex, still others material possessions. The list is almost endless. I think of Harris Johnson's old hymn "Some folks would rather have houses and land, some folks choose silver and gold. These things they treasure, and forget their souls. I've decided to make Jesus my choice." Put your trust in Jesus. Jesus is God's answer to our need. Jesus is God's "yes" for our today. Jesus, the one who was, the one who is to come, the one who is.

The Gospel—the good news of Christ—tells us that Jesus, the Savior, is God's presence for life today. He is present to touch us in today's pain, in today's depression, in today's anxieties, in today's decisions—whatever our today may bring. Not only must we ask him, we must trust and believe that he can help us.

Jesus cares about people no matter who they are, what they are, or where they are in life. Jesus, the Savior, meets us where we are—in our ups and downs. He meets us in our peaks and valleys. He meets us in our joys and sorrows. He meets us in our pain or pleasure. No one is outside the circle of his love. Jesus Christ, the one who was, the one who will come again, the one who is—our Savior in our today.

Some of us know this. If we were a testifying church, some of us could raise that old gospel hymn as our own personal testimony:

Somebody sought me, when I was wandering
Out in the desert, all laden with sin
Somebody spoke to me, and with compassion
Said to me gently, "sinner come on in."
Somebody heard me when I was praying;
Somebody touched me while passing by;
Somebody told me, be not discouraged;
Somebody gave me the courage to try.
Somebody sought me when I was sinking;
Somebody rescued my soul from the grave;
Somebody folded me close to his bosom;
O! It was Jesus. He's mighty to save.
(source unknown)

We all can come to the point where a particular or peculiar circumstance seems beyond our ability to master. Similarly we may find ourselves in a situation about which we feel we can't talk, or we feel nobody would understand our distress. The next time you face such a dilemma and can't seem to find a solution—take it Jesus. The Savior is there with an answer.

Some say, I don't know how to pray. Conversation with Jesus does not call for great oratory or high intellectual discourse. The dying thief on Calvary said only, "Jesus, remember me when you come into your kingdom," and he was promised paradise that very day. (Lk. 24:42) You can search out the Savior in the pages of Holy Writ. He is there from beginning to end. "In the beginning was the Word, and the Word was with God and the Word was God." (Jn. 1:1) And if you trace that Word all the way through our "source book," the Bible, you will find that, according to one writer (and I have long-forgotten the source):

In Genesis, he's the seed of the woman
In Exodus, he's the Passover lamb
In Leviticus, he's the atoning sacrifice
In Numbers, he's the smitten rock
In Deuteronomy, he's the prophet
In Joshua, he's the captain
In Judges, he's the deliverer
In Ruth, he's the kinsman
In Kings, he's the ruler
In Nehemiah, he's the restorer
In Esther, he's the advocate
In Job, he's the redeemer
In Psalms, he's the shepherd
In Proverbs, he's wisdom
In Ecclesiastes, he's the goal
In the Song of Solomon, he's the groom
In the Prophets, he's the coming one
In the Gospels, he's the God made man
In Acts, he's the risen one
In the Epistles, he's the head of the church and
In Revelation, he's the worthy one

If you are looking for a savior, his name is
Jesus—the one who was, the one who is to come,
the one who is. And, as the writer of the letter to

the Hebrews tells us (Heb. 13:8), "Jesus Christ is the same yesterday and today and forever."

Amen.

VI

Easter Grace in a Good Friday World

A confirmation sermon following
September 11, 2001

John 11:25-26

I thank God for the opportunity to be with you today as we all try to wrap our minds around the events of this past Tuesday and the way in which most, if not all of us, have been touched and effected by these tragedies, either directly or indirectly. I certainly am aware of how this parish has been effected. Your bishops are holding you in prayer. (Bishop Tom Shaw SSJE, stranded overseas, particularly wants you to know of his concern as he tries desperately to return home early from his sabbatical pilgrimage in Turkey and Greece. Please keep him in your prayers.) As we welcome into fuller fellowship through this Sacrament of Confirmation, young people who, for the most part, have never known national disaster, we are painfully aware that horrific acts, unprecedented on our own soil and in our immediate sight, have shaken us to our core.

As we reflect on what happened last Tuesday—each in our own way, we may be tempted to question why so many innocent lives and symbols of our way of life could be destroyed in almost the twinkling of the eye. And what are we to make of the unfortunate ramifications of that disaster? I am not sure there are either pat or satisfactory answers to such questions, nor perhaps do there need to be at that particular level. We should have an even deeper question on our hearts this day and that is: What is the source of our inner strength in times like these? What enables and empowers us to make sense of our own lives and to make the rest of our lives worth living?

For me, at least, a part of the answer comes from the eleventh chapter of the Gospel according to John. Jesus says to Martha, "I am the resurrection and the life. Those who believe in me, even though they die, will live, and everyone who lives and believes in me will never die." (Jn. 11:25–26) This brief exchange between Jesus and Martha of Bethany catches the attention, captures the imagination, and calls forth in us a sense of hope. And, indeed, as Christians, we are prisoners of hope. We are Easter people. We are Easter people in a Good Friday world.

The world is full of the misery and the pain of Good Friday. We have only to open our daily newspapers, turn on the television to the nightly news or, as we did on Tuesday past, turn on the "breaking" news for fresh reminders of the violence, cruelty, want, and need that permeates our world. We have only to examine and reflect on our own lives, our own trials and tribulations, our own cares and woes. We have only to consider how we relate to each other and to our world neighbors. But we are Easter people, and we are *supposed* to be different.

There are some distinctive characteristics about Easter people that keep us in close touch with this Jesus who says to a grieving Martha: "I am the resurrection and the life. Those who believe in me, even though they die, will live, and everyone who lives and believes in me will never die.

Easter people are believers. We believe not only in the possible, we believe also in the *im*possible. We believe that the lame were made to walk, and the mute made to speak, that lepers were cleansed and the blind received their sight. If we can believe that Jesus, who died, rose again from the dead, and ascended to be with God, his Father, then we can, in peace, give over those who have died—known and unknown—to a loving, compassionate and ever merciful God who has prepared for us a better home than this Good Friday world. For did Jesus not say: "Do not your hearts be troubled. Believe in God, believe also in me. In my Father's house there are many dwelling places. If it were not so, would I have told you that I go to prepare a place for you...so that where I am, there you may be also." (Jn. 14:1-3)

And so we can believe also that with the helpful presence of God's Holy Spirit, we are strengthened and sustained on our earthly pilgrimage. Further, we can believe that we can fashion new lives committed to love, to peace, to justice, and to liberation for all of God's people.

Easter people grieve and need to be comforted. And, yes, Easter people get angry. Many are angry about the devastation events of Tuesday's attack and its aftermath. But we must seek to channel that anger in constructive ways. Be angry enough to say and to seriously mean, I will commit my life to living out the Baptismal Covenant: seeking and serving Christ in all persons, loving my neighbor as myself, striving for justice and peace among all people, respecting the dignity of every human being.

Easter people hang in until the end. Like the women who stood by the cross, Easter people live by the words of the old spiritual: "I will go, I shall go to see what the end will be." For as Easter people, we have, indeed, come this far by faith, and we trust our God for the next step of the journey. Easter people share. We share sorrow as well as joy; good times as well as bad; mountaintop highs and wilderness woes. For to share only life's bright side is to deny the reality of the human condition. To share only the lovely is to leave ourselves unprepared for our own Good Fridays and unable to support others in theirs.

Easter people not only bear the sign of the cross on their brow, their lives bear the marks of the Gospel and the fruit of the Spirit. The fruit of the Spirit, the apostle Paul tells us, is love, joy, peace, patience, kindness, generosity, faithfulness, gentleness, and self-control.

What is the source of our inner strength? What enables and empowers us? Grace!

That amazing grace that supported Job throughout his travail and woe, allowing him to proclaim, "I know that my Redeemer lives, and that at the last he will stand upon the earth; and after my skin has been thus destroyed, then in my flesh I shall see God . . . and my eyes shall behold, and not another." (Job 14:26-27) The amazing grace that raised a song in Mary's heart when she was told she would bear the Son of God. "My soul magnifies the Lord, and my spirit rejoices in God my Savior . . . ." (Lk. 1:46-47)

Grace moved John Newton, onetime captain of a slave ship, weary of trafficking in human flesh. After much effort he became a priest of the church and gave us that great hymn to which we so often turn for comfort, "Amazing grace, how sweet the sound." It is grace that supports us "through many dangers, toils, and snares." It is grace that will see us as individuals, as families, as congregations, as a diocese, as a church, as a commonwealth, and as a nation through this great grief and loss. And it is that same grace—God's amazing grace—that will continue to strengthen and sustain us as Easter people in this Good Friday world.

VII

Costly Friendship

*A sermon for the Feast of Saint Simon and
Saint Jude, at the Society of Saint John the
Evangelist, Cambridge, Massachusetts*

John 15:17–27

Here this evening we observe the feast of
Saints Simon and Jude, about whom little
factual information is generally known. By tradition and through the Collect for the feast, however, we are told that they were faithful and zealous
in their mission—bearing witness to Christ as
apostles to Persia. It is to such faithful and zealous

witness that Jesus called his disciples in the appointed reading from the Gospel according to John. A faithful and zealous witness that would be neither easy nor by any means all sweetness and light. Rather, it would be a sojourn fraught with hostility, hatred, and the possibility of martyrdom so many instances of which have made our history. From Peter, who begged to crucified upside down because he declared himself unworthy to die in the same manner as Jesus, to "your own" Bernard Mizeki, who was converted to faith in Jesus Christ by the witness of missionaries from the SSJE and who died at the point of the spear for his belief. The phrase "I never promised you a rose garden" might well have been coined by our Lord.

The disciples were invited by anointment and appointment into a sacrificial and costly friendship with Jesus. They were told that because of him, they would encounter hostility and hatred. If, said Jesus, you were of the world, the world would love you as its own. But I chose you *out* of the world to stand, as it were, *against* the preoccupations of the world. Therefore, the world is going to hate you. Not a very enticing invitation to continued discipleship or ministry. Not much of an inducement to "go ye into all the world and make disciples of all nations," et cetera, especially in light of this invitation's being one of their Master's farewell discourses. What a dismal prospect! What an unsolicitous bidding! Who would want or need it!

"You did not choose me but I chose you. And I appointed you to go and bear fruit, fruit that will last," says Jesus. And we have seen the fruit of those laborers, the earliest friends of Jesus, such apostles as Simon and Jude, and countless others throughout the ages—even some known to us in our own day.

We, too, are called into a costly and sacrificial friendship with Jesus. A friendship that, as the apostle Paul admonishes, requires "speaking the truth in love." A friendship that risks hostility whether by questioning the validity of our government's gearing up the machines of war for a dubious crusade, by challenging the policies of an allied nation that maintains a civilian army of occupation on the hills of Zion and rumbles its tanks into the very birthplace of our Lord, or even by standing up against the materialistic and individualistic trappings of this world and taking vows of poverty, celibacy, and obedience. Yes, even those who choose and profess the religious life can become objects of scorn and derision because they are an unpleasant reminder of what a real walk with Christ can be.

Indeed, any of us can encounter hostility and hatred when we stand in true friendship with and witness to Christ. Real relationship with Christ is a fearsome thing. For having seen what the love of Christ can do in transforming the lives of people—work we are called to emulate—we find that the ways of the world seem less risky, less costly, less self-effacing, less sacrificial, and certainly far more attractive. I think of the work this commu-

nity has done over the years—against overwhelm-
ing odds—to rescue and redeem the lives of inner-
city children at risk. I think back also to the familiar words from our gospel lesson of two Sundays
ago when we observed the annual Children's Sabbath weekend. "Give therefore to the emperor the
things that are the emperor's and to God the
things that are God's." (Mt. 22:21)

In an open letter to all faith communities,
Marian Wright Edelman, founder and president of
the Children's Defense Fund, which sponsors the
Children's Sabbath wrote, in part, "The breach of
hunger and homelessness and lack of health care
hinders millions of children from learning and developing to their full potential. Growling tummies,
exhaustion from chaotic homeless-shelter life and
untreated illness distract children from learning
and make their focus just surviving one more day.
It is time to repair the breach of hunger and homelessness. When congregations and communities
come together to serve and seek justice for chil-

dren, they are repairing the breach and raising up the foundations of future generations."

As I frequently have mentioned, many resist the notion that civic and social responsibility fall within the purview of the faith community. Others raise such questions as, What should be the church's stance toward the affairs of state and the leaders of the nation? While we yearn for easy answers to complicated questions and "sound bite" solutions to complex problems, Jesus appeals to us to look beyond the simplistic politics and legalisms of Caesar's coin and realize that we are called to embrace the values of a faith that, as one writer put it, "sees the hand of God in all things and every human being as part of a single family under the providence of God."

If that for which we so fervently pray—peace, justice, human wholeness, and unity—is to become reality, then people of faith must help by living out their faith in the public arena, where the risk of hostility and hatred are palpable. Along with Jesus' dire warning to the disciples, there is a word of encouragement and empowerment. "When the Advocate comes, whom I will send to you from the Father, the Spirit of truth who comes from the Father, he will testify on my behalf." The disciples also had been told, among other things, "if you ask anything of the Father in my name, he will give it you."

But beyond the dire warnings and the words of encouragement found throughout these several farewell discourses, of which our gospel lesson is but one, there have been and there are people—even those who had or who have trouble accepting Jesus—as scripture tells us, who "were astonished at his teaching, for he taught them as one having authority, and not as the scribes." (Mk. 1:22)

A question for us in the face of hostility and hatred is, Do we ever astonish anybody by our witness? Or is our witness so bland as to be of the tepid nature that moved Jesus himself was to say, "So, because you are lukewarm, and neither cold

not hot, I am about to spit you out of my mouth"
Do we ever by risky, sacrificial, *costly* friendship
with Jesus astonish anybody? Would to God that
we might! Amen.

VIII

Parting Words

An address to the Diocesan Convention,
Boston, Massachusetts, November 2002

Mark 4:35–41

We gather in convention on the Feast of All Saints, a day on which we are reminded of our linkage with those holy women and men who have gone before us, those who are with us, and those who will follow after us. And while it is rightly a time for recollection for all of us, is it a peculiar and particular time of reflection for me as

I entertain the twin thoughts of the luxury of not having to rise at six in the morning, and the strange and sobering prospect of no longer being personally engaged with the people of this great diocese as your bishop suffragan.

Briefly, then, I want to share with you some thoughts, some parting words, on the latter reality in light of the Gospel lesson from Matthew which we will hear today in the Eucharist—the familiar Beatitudes from the Sermon on the Mount. This passage holds up for us the qualities of Christian discipleship to which we are all called by baptism. As I have haltingly and imperfectly tried to live into the promises and challenges of the Beatitudes as your bishop, the remarks made just prior to my consecration by two of my role models still ring in my ears. As I was preparing to leave Philadelphia, the Reverend Audrey Bronson—now a bishop in a Pentecostal fellowship of churches, and who, along with Harriet Tubman and Tina Turner, is one of my heroines—admonished me, "The power behind you is greater than the task ahead of you!" Her words have certainly proven true over these past thirteen-plus years, because without question, the power of God's Holy Spirit, working through you and others in the church, has guided and sustained my ministry among you.

It was the Spirit who guided and sustained me through those early days when, as a woman in the House of Bishops, I was treading the winepress alone, until I was at last joined by Jane Dixon of Washington, D.C., and later, by Mary Adelia McLeod of Vermont. Over time, others joined us, one by one. It is interesting to note that at my consecration there were two lengthy objections; at Jane's, there were also two; at Mary Adelia's, there was one—and there have been none since. This says something about the church's growth on the subject of women in the episcopate. It is no longer an aberration, but a reality of the church's life. As the House of Bishops no longer sits in order of consecration, it is now possible to look over that gathering in any direction and see a woman. It is with great satisfaction, then, that I move into retirement with nine—soon to be ten—sisters in the House.

Likewise, it was the Spirit who guided and sustained me through a time when there was a calculated effort to neutralize my influence and to mute my voice here in this diocese. But I have always been, as you know, a firm believer in poetic sentiment, and particularly that expressed by gospel song writer, Thomas A. Dorsey, "When the load bears down so heavy, the weight is shown upon your brow, there a sweet relief in knowing, the Lord will make a way somehow."

Since Bishop Bronson's words have rung so true in my ministry, I gladly offer her admonition to you—particularly as you as a diocese move toward a new and richer strategy for mission in the months ahead. "The power behind you is greater than the task ahead of you." I am confident that this diocese will grow in grace as you develop new approaches to the vital ministries already taking place, and as you respond to the new opportunities and challenges that the Spirit of truth will reveal to you.

At dinner on the eve of my consecration the Reverend Doctor Van Samuel Bird, my chief tutor and true mentor, remarked, "God does not always—or even *usually*—call us because we are finished products or perfect instruments for his service. God calls us, then remolds, equips, and empowers us for his service. Not only do we have this treasure in earthen vessels (as Paul reminds us), but when the vessel becomes cracked or marred, God, like a potter, does not cast it away. God reshapes it into a new vessel, as Jeremiah tells us."

And so for these past thirteen-plus years, if there has been one watchword on my lips it has been, "Please be patient with me, 'cause God is not through with me yet." And God still is not finished with me. Nor is God through with *any* of us yet. So I pray that you will continue to go from strength to strength, in God's joyful service as you are reshaped, remolded, reequipped, and re-empowered in the days and weeks and months and years ahead.

No reflection of my ministry among you would be complete without citing some high points along the way, and certainly there have been many. The partnership forged with Bishop Tom Shaw, SSJE has been a high water mark for me. This team ministry and personal friendship we have been privileged to share over the course of his episcopate has been a blessing I scarcely deserve, but it is one for which I shall be eternally grateful. I recall telling this convention when Tom was elected to be mindful of the fact that he is a good man and a holy man, but he is *just* a man. He was not going to save the world—or this diocese— overnight. As great as I think he is, and as much as I love him, what I said then is still true today. He should not be looked to alone, or even in company with bishops Bud Cedarholm and Gayle Harris, for the health and welfare of this diocese.

I also would have to say how it has been gratifying to see the climate of the Diocese of Massachusetts change so dramatically, from one of mistrust and individualism to a more common fellowship where our congregations, clergy, diocesan staff, and organizations and agencies such as Episcopal City Mission and the Union of Black Episcopalians (to name but two) have moved into closer relationship and ownership of a shared ministry. *And* like the ad Virginia Slims cigarettes says, "You've come a long way, baby!" But baby, you've still got a long way to go.

And, of course, a high point for me was simply being with you in the places where as clergy and people you do ministry. I have not spent as much time as I should have or would have like to have spent with our extra-parochial and retired clergy, but I have had the good fortune to visit all but two of our congregations and to exercise a sacramental ministry in all but three. When I recall the fact that on May 1, 1842, Alexander Crummell—a black man—was ordained deacon in Saint Paul's Cathedral by Bishop Alexander Griswold, and that it took another 121 years before Massachusetts ordained a black priest in 1963, I remind myself that, perhaps, as a black and as a woman, I haven't done too badly.

Then there were all the humorous moments, most of which were provided by the knowing observations and canny comments of our diocesan children. At the reception on a recent parish visitation, a little girl of about five was waiting, not too patiently, for someone to cut the cake so that she could get her slice and go home. She finally figured out that no one was going to move toward the cake as long as I was entertaining questions from those who had gathered in the parish hall. When I asked if there was a final question, she raised her precious little hand and asked, "When are you leaving?"

Another girl child, about four years old, on seeing me attired in my turquoise cope and miter, inquired in a loud, husky voice, "Is that the queen?" Throughout the service she repeatedly informed her parents—in that same loud, throaty tone—"I want to go sit with the queen!" Not to be outdone, a four-year old boy looked at me and asked his father, "Is she a pirate?" On being told no, he then demanded to know, "Well, why is she wearing a pirate's hat?"

And just as there have peaks, there have been some valleys. I won't dwell on those here because you will then have heard a portion of the book I'm writing, and you would not then have to buy it! And if you just hold out a little longer until further senility sets in, you probably will hear some of the same stories repeated several times over anyway.

I will say, however, that in those dark and painful moments of hate mail, death threats, and the ire of various detractors, in those days of living in a fish bowl where it seemed that my every word and move was scrutinized, I had the wise counsel of the quintessential confidant, ally, and supporter, Canon Ed Rodman. It was he who advised me among other things, not to take it personally and to remember that "it gets worse when the Red Sox are losing." Thank you, Rod, for being there through thick and thin, in good times and bad. I want to say thanks, also, to the many of you who have sent cards, notes, and letters in recent days to say what my ministry has meant to you personally. Thanks to the Massachusetts Episcopal Clergy Association and to the many congregations for your kind remembrances.

I cannot close without saying that the Diocese of Massachusetts took an enormous, incredible, and courageous risk on September 25, 1988, in electing me. You took on what could have been a tremendous liability, not even knowing if the Standing Committees and/or bishops of this church would consent to such an election. It was touch and go for a while, even after the great celebration at the Hynes Auditorium on February 11, 1989, as some waited for the train wreck to occur. The Episcopal Synod (now Forward in Faith, North America) declared, "The final crisis has come upon the Episcopal Church..." I can only hope that in some small way your temerity and your audacity of faith have been vindicated.

In my recent visitations I have been telling folk there is a new Bishop Harris coming on the scene, and I do mean new. Furthermore, as some of you have already heard me say, she is twenty-one years younger than I, she is twenty-one years smarter than I, she is twenty-one years better looking than I, and she sings twenty-one times better than I do. I hope you will embrace and affirm her ministry as you have embraced, affirmed, and supported mine over our time together.

Blessed are you, pure in heart. Thanks for a great ride. And thanks be to God who gives us the victory through our Lord Jesus Christ. Amen.

Afterword

The Power Behind—
The Task Ahead

*A pastoral charge at the ordination and
consecration of Gayle Elizabeth Harris
as bishop suffragan of the Diocese of
Massachusetts, January 18, 2003*

My sister Gayle Elizabeth, it is my great
privilege to deliver a few personal
words to you as you enter a new phase of ministry to which the people of the Diocese of
Massachusetts and the Holy Spirit have called
you. Our brother, Bishop Chester Talton, has
inspired and lifted us up in his preaching of the

Gospel; I will now bring us—and particularly *you*—back down to earth.

Each time I have the opportunity to deliver a charge at a consecration, I find myself offering some of the same admonitions. But not this time. No, today, I have a new sense of Denis Wortman's familiar ordination hymn, "God of the prophets, bless the prophet's heirs; Elijah's mantle o're Elisha is cast. Each age for thine own solemn task prepare. Make each one stronger, nobler than the last." As a black woman, you know, in the timeless words of "Lift every voice and sing," that you have "come over a way that with tears has been watered." You know that you have "come treading your path through the blood of the slaughtered." And we know it, too.

Soon the bishops here present, acting for the community of faith, will set their seal upon you. You will be charged, ordained, and entrusted with a new and wider ministry, to which you bring your unique gifts and a demonstrated love for God's people. You have enjoyed a rich and varied ministry in parishes and in the dioceses of Newark, Washington, and Rochester. But not much that you have done in the past specifically prepares you for some of the challenges you will face in the days ahead. In the weeks and days preceding this glorious day, working in the diocesan offices, you have already tasted some of the sadder duties of the episcopate and the heartaches it can bring. You will, however, come to know the joyful work of this office as well. Through it all, remember *who* you are and *whose* are and that you come among God's people to serve them by enabling their ministries.

During your examination you will be asked, among other things, if you will boldly proclaim and interpret the Gospel of Christ, enlightening the minds and stirring up the conscience of your people. And your response must be, "I will, in the power of the Spirit." Your best efforts in this regard, however, will not always be understood—or welcomed. In both word and deed, you must proclaim redemption, liberation, hope, and love. And you must also proclaim judgment, reminding us that we cannot go back to the garden of Eden but instead must step into the new age, not knowing what its final shape will be. But we have come "this far by faith," and we trust our God for the next step of the journey.

You must not demur from urging us out of the comfortable pew and challenging us to seek the welfare of the city and the suburbs alike, for the problems of the city eventually become the problems of those suburban communities. In this complex and diverse diocese, on some days you will see your role with great clarity, and you may be tempted to sing with Professor Henry Higgins in *My Fair Lady*, "I've got it! By Jove, I think I've got it!" And on others (probably more numerous), you will feel like you are trying to put pantyhose on an octopus.

Shortly, in addition to the Holy Scriptures, from which you will be charged to feed and nurture the flock of Christ, you will be presented with some symbols of your office as bishop. Remember, they are only symbols. They point to a deeper reality of life, but they are *not* the reality of life. You will receive a ring, a symbol of authority—but it is only a ring. It is not your life. Your authority demands integrity, accountability, and service. You will receive a staff, a sign of the shepherd's office. The shepherd's responsibility entails endless care of the flock entrusted to the shepherd's charge. But remember, it is a staff only, a symbol. It is not your life. A miter will be placed on your head as a crown of fire, evocative of the flames of the Spirit which fell unbidden upon the disciples on the day of Pentecost. It, too, is symbolic; it is *only* a miter. *It is not your life!*

No. Remember this: it is *prayer* that is your life and *prayer* that is your life-line. Your mentor and mine, the late John Thomas Walker exhorted Allen Batlett at his consecration some seventeen years ago, "Pray often, sing when you can, weep daily over the city, and wash the feet of the weak and the lowly, the black and the white, the poor and the rich, the sick and the healthy, the believer and the unbeliever." And let this old gospel hymn be the substance of your prayer as a bishop in the Church of God:

> *I come to thee my Savior for strength to do thy*
> *   will.*
> *I ask of thee a favor: the strength to do thy will.*
> *I need thy rich anointing that those in bonds*
> *   may be*
> *Delivered and inspired, comforted and set free.*
> *Consecrate me, consecrate me, consecrate me to*
> *   do thy will.*
> *Consecrate me, consecrate me, consecrate me to*
> *   do thy will.*

God bless you, my sister, and may you go from strength to strength in Christ's joyful service, knowing and never forgetting that "the power behind you is greater than the task ahead of you."